ARIZONA
CARDINALS

by Marty Gitlin

Published by ABDO Publishing Company, 8000 West 78th Street, Edina, Minnesota 55439. Copyright © 2011 by Abdo Consulting Group, Inc. International copyrights reserved in all countries. No part of this book may be reproduced in any form without written permission from the publisher. SportsZone™ is a trademark and logo of ABDO Publishing Company.

Printed in the United States of America,
North Mankato, Minnesota
062010
092010

 THIS BOOK CONTAINS AT LEAST 10% RECYCLED MATERIALS.

Editor: Matt Tustison
Copy Editor: Nicholas Cafarelli
Interior Design and Production: Kazuko Collins
Cover Design: Craig Hinton

Photo Credits: Paul Jasienski/AP Images, cover; AP Images, title page, 12, 15, 18, 20, 28, 31, 42 (middle); Rob Schumacher/AP Images, 4, 34, 43 (middle); Mark J. Terrill/AP Images, 7, 11; David J. Phillip/AP Images, 9; Harry L. Hall/AP Images, 17, 42 (top); NFL Photos/AP Images, 22, 24, 27, 42 (bottom), 43 (top), 44; Chad Surmick/AP Images, 32; East Valley Tribune, Brian Fitzgerald/AP Images, 37; Jeff Roberson/AP Images, 39, 43 (bottom); Matt York/AP Images, 41; Ross D. Franklin/AP Images, 47

Library of Congress Cataloging-in-Publication Data
Gitlin, Marty.
 Arizona Cardinals / Marty Gitlin.
  p. cm. — (Inside the NFL)
 Includes index.
 ISBN 978-1-61714-001-3   48 : ILL (cc)
 1. Arizona Cardinals (Football team)—History—Juvenile literature. I. Title.
 GV956.A75G57 2011
 796.332'6409791—dc22
               2010013671

TABLE OF CONTENTS

CHAPTER 1

SUPER BOWL! FINALLY!

The last time the Cardinals had played for a National Football League (NFL) title, a new invention called television was all the rage. It was 1948.

When the 2008 regular season concluded, it did not seem as if Arizona should be eagerly preparing to celebrate a championship. Sure, the Cardinals qualified for the playoffs. But they barely did. Arizona was blown out twice in the final three weeks of the regular season. This included a 47–7 loss to the New England Patriots. The Cardinals sneaked into the

NUMBERS CAN LIE

It is not surprising that few fans and sports media members believed that the 2008 Cardinals could reach the Super Bowl with their defense. After all, they gave up an average of 26.6 points per game during the regular season. They surrendered 56 points in one game against the New York Jets, 48 points in another against Philadelphia, and 47 in yet another against New England. The Cardinals collectively outscored their opponents by just one point (427–426) in 16 games before the playoffs. But the team got hot just in time.

TERRELLE SMITH (45) AND GABE WATSON BECOME EMOTIONAL AFTER ARIZONA ADVANCED TO THE SUPER BOWL WITH A 32–25 WIN OVER PHILADELPHIA ON JANUARY 18, 2009.

LEAPING LARRY

After the 2008 season, the Cardinals' Larry Fitzgerald had the finest playoff run ever for a wide receiver. In four games, including the Super Bowl, he caught 30 passes for 546 yards and seven touchdowns. All three numbers set NFL postseason records.

Fitzgerald took the league by storm after joining the Cardinals in 2004. He caught 523 passes for 7,067 yards and 59 touchdowns from 2004 to 2009. He led the NFL in catches in 2005 and in touchdowns in 2008 and 2009.

His success stems greatly from his work ethic and passion for the game. He admits he sometimes goes too far, though.

"When I'm not doing something well, or I didn't play my best, it kind of eats at me," he said. "... My love for this sport is definitely a sickness. It's one of my best attributes, but at the wrong time, it can be one of my worst attributes."

postseason with a 9–7 record. Their defense was not exactly frightening opponents. In addition, they would have to win three games to qualify for their first Super Bowl. Their chances seemed slim.

Then a strange thing happened. The defense began to perform better than it had all year. The Cardinals held down the Atlanta Falcons' explosive offense in the first round of the playoffs. They stuffed the Falcons' running game and intercepted two passes in a 30–24 home victory. They followed it up with their best defensive game of the season. They recorded five interceptions in a surprisingly lopsided

THE CARDINALS' LARRY FITZGERALD MAKES A JUMPING CATCH IN FRONT OF THE EAGLES' ASANTE SAMUEL DURING THE NFC CHAMPIONSHIP GAME IN JANUARY 2009.

33–13 win over the host Carolina Panthers.

Now anything seemed possible. The Cardinals hosted the National Football Conference (NFC) Championship Game against the Philadelphia Eagles. They had a chance to make a Super Bowl dream come true. But that wonderful dream appeared to be turning into a nightmare when the Eagles scored three second-half touchdowns to take a 25–24 lead.

That is when veteran Cardinals quarterback Kurt Warner was at his best. He drove his team 72 yards down the field and threw a touchdown pass to running back Tim Hightower to clinch a 32–25 victory. The dream was reality. The Cardinals were in the Super Bowl.

"I always dreamed it, and it's finally here," Cardinals Pro Bowl safety Adrian Wilson said. "The Arizona Cardinals changed their stripes today. Nobody gave us a chance; nobody gave this organization a chance."

Few gave them a chance to defeat the tough Pittsburgh Steelers in the Super Bowl, either. But Warner and the wide receiver trio of Larry Fitzgerald, Anquan Boldin, and

THE MAIN MAN

The Cardinals were struggling heading into 2008. But the hiring of Ken Whisenhunt as coach played a major role in the team's turnaround. Whisenhunt guided the team to an 8–8 record in 2007 before taking it to the Super Bowl a year later. In 2009, the Cardinals won 10 games for the first time since 1976. They reached the second round of the playoffs before falling to eventual Super Bowl champion New Orleans.

ARIZONA'S KURT WARNER THROWS AGAINST PITTSBURGH DURING SUPER BOWL XLIII. WARNER PASSED FOR 377 YARDS AND THREE TOUCHDOWNS.

Steve Breaston helped the Cardinals take a 23–20 lead late in the game. Fitzgerald scored two touchdowns, including a go-ahead 64-yard reception with 2:37 left.

It was one of the most thrilling finishes in Super Bowl history—and it came down to the final minute. But when Steelers quarterback Ben Roethlisberger fired a 6-yard touchdown pass to wide receiver Santonio Holmes in the corner of the end zone with 35 seconds remaining, the Cardinals were finished.

The game was lost 27–23, but the Cardinals were not losers. "I am so proud to be a part of this football team," Warner said after the game. "I think that is one of the reasons why [the defeat] doesn't hurt as bad as it could. These guys have exceeded expectations."

Low expectations for the Cardinals had been established decades before the team arrived in Arizona.

RARE ACHIEVEMENT

The 2008 Cardinals became only the fifth team in NFL history to feature three players with 1,000 receiving yards in one season. Wide receivers Larry Fitzgerald (1,431 yards), Anquan Boldin (1,038 yards), and Steve Breaston (1,006 yards) all exceeded that milestone.

THE CARDINALS' LARRY FITZGERALD BREAKS AWAY FOR A 64-YARD TOUCHDOWN RECEPTION IN SUPER BOWL XLIII.

CHAPTER 2

EARLY SUCCESSES, EARLY FAILURES

Those who think the Cardinals are fairly new because they arrived in Arizona in 1988 will have to think again.

When the Cardinals franchise was born, the president of the United States was William McKinley, radio had yet to be invented, and the country was involved in the Spanish-American War.

The Cardinals landed in Arizona in 1988. But it was in 1898 when a neighborhood

A "NORMAL" NICKNAME?

Around the turn of the twentieth century, the team now known as the Cardinals boasted a very unusual nickname. It was called the Normals. Why? Because it played its games at Normal Field, which rested on the South Side of Chicago. In 1901, however, the team began to wear uniforms that owner Chris O'Brien considered to be cardinal red. He then changed the name to the Cardinals.

CHICAGO CARDINALS OWNER CHARLES W. BIDWILL, *RIGHT*, HANDS NEW COACH JIMMY CONZELMAN A CONTRACT IN 1940. AS OF 2010, THE BIDWILL FAMILY STILL OWNED THE CARDINALS.

team representing the Morgan Athletic Club began competing in Chicago. Three years later, the "Cardinals" nickname was adopted. But the team disbanded in 1906 because there were simply not enough opponents against whom to compete.

The Cardinals returned in 1913. They captured the Chicago Football League title in 1917. In 1920, they joined the American Professional Football Association, which became the NFL two years later.

The Cardinals quickly established themselves as one of the premier teams in the NFL. They finished with nonlosing records in each of their first six seasons. They won the league championship in 1925 by compiling an 11–2–1 record. Since there were no playoffs until 1933, that regular-season mark was good enough to earn them the crown.

SEEN ON RACINE

Until 1922, the Cardinals were known as the Racine Cardinals. The team did not play in Racine, Wisconsin. But it did play on the corner of Sixty-first and Racine in Chicago. Racine is one of the main streets in the city.

Chicago doctor David Jones bought the team in 1929 and signed fullback Ernie Nevers, its first star player. Nevers made an immediate impact on Thanksgiving Day that same year. He scored an NFL-record 40 points with six touchdowns and four extra points in a 40–6 win over the archrival Chicago Bears. The game was billed as a showdown between Nevers and Bears star Red Grange.

Jones sold the team to Charles W. Bidwill in 1932. This started the current period of Bidwill family ownership. But the purchase did not begin an era of prosperity. The

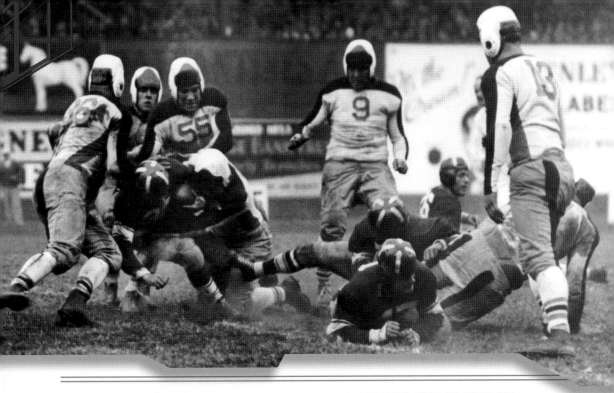

THE CHICAGO CARDINALS' IKE PETERSON RUNS AGAINST THE GIANTS ON OCTOBER 27, 1935, IN NEW YORK. THE CARDINALS WENT 6–4–2 IN 1935.

Cardinals enjoyed a winning season in 1935, and then collapsed. They compiled a record of 12–70–3 from 1938 to 1945. In the last three of those seasons, they were a miserable 1–29. They failed to win any games in 1943 or 1944.

One reason for those failures was that the Cardinals lost more players to military service during World War II than most

NEVERS BETTER

The Cardinals were fortunate to eventually land fullback Ernie Nevers after his standout college career at Stanford University. He was also a fine baseball and basketball player who signed professional contracts in those sports. Nevers began his pro football career with the Duluth Eskimos in 1926. They actually changed their name to the "Ernie Nevers Eskimos" in his honor. He played three years with the Cardinals, from 1929 to 1931. He was an All-Pro selection in each of those seasons. Nevers found far less success in his one year coaching the team, compiling a 1–10 record in 1939.

A MAN OF DEDICATION

The Chicago Cardinals were among the NFL's worst teams during the ownership period of Charles W. Bidwill. The squad was even overshadowed in its own town by the more successful Chicago Bears. In 1946, further competition arose when the All-America Football Conference was formed and put a team called the Rockets in that city.

Bidwill lost money every season he owned the Cardinals from 1933 through 1946. He loved football. But he also wanted to win. So in 1947 he outbid the Rockets for the services of University of Georgia running back Charley Trippi. Bidwill signed Trippi to a contract worth $100,000, an unheard-of amount at that time.

The Cardinals were finally ready to win. But Bidwill died in April 1947, just after he had compiled a championship-caliber squad. His wife, Violet, assumed control of the team for the next 15 years.

of the other NFL teams. Among those players were quarterback Johnny Clement, wide receiver Billy Dewell, and lineman Joe Kuharich.

But in the NFL, teams can transform themselves into big winners in a hurry. And two years after being the laughingstock of the league, the Cardinals were world champions. Little could anyone suspect, however, that more than 60 years later, the team would still be seeking its next NFL title.

CARDINALS OWNER CHARLES W. BIDWILL, *LEFT*, RUNNING BACK CHARLEY TRIPPI, AND COACH JIMMY CONZELMAN CHAT AFTER TRIPPI SIGNED A FOUR-YEAR, $100,000 CONTRACT IN 1947.

EARLY SUCCESSES, EARLY FAILURES **17**

CHAPTER 3

A TITLE, STRUGGLE, AND MOVE

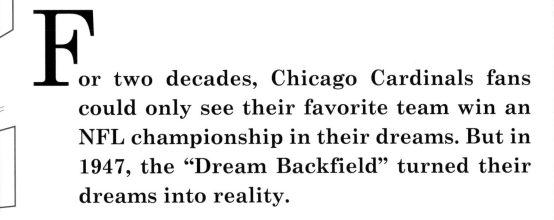

For two decades, Chicago Cardinals fans could only see their favorite team win an NFL championship in their dreams. But in 1947, the "Dream Backfield" turned their dreams into reality.

The Dream Backfield was also known as the "Million Dollar Backfield." It consisted of quarterback Paul Christman and running backs Pat Harder, Elmer Angsman, and Charley Trippi. The quartet performed brilliantly that season for coach and future Pro Football Hall of Fame inductee Jimmy Conzelman.

TWO TRAGEDIES IN TWO YEARS

In October 1947, Cardinals rookie punter Jeff Burkett was killed in a plane crash in Utah. He was leading the NFL in punting average at the time. The tragedy forced Charley Trippi to take over the punting duties. He later said that he thought about Burkett every time he dropped back to punt. The next year, Cardinals tackle Stan Mauldin died of a heart attack in the locker room after the first game of the 1948 season.

FROM *LEFT*, THE CARDINALS' ELMER ANGSMAN, PAUL CHRISTMAN, AND PAT HARDER TAKE TO THE AIR AT TRAINING CAMP IN AUGUST 1948.

CARDINALS COACH JIMMY CONZELMAN RUBS THE HEADS OF CHARLEY TRIPPI, *RIGHT*, AND ELMER ANGSMAN AS ASSISTANT COACH PHIL HANDLER GRINS AFTER CHICAGO'S 1947 NFL TITLE GAME WIN.

Fueled by the Dream Backfield and a strong defense, the Cardinals raced out to a 7–1 start. They finished 9–3 and clinched a title game showdown in Chicago against the Philadelphia Eagles.

The heroes of the regular season proved to be the heroes of the championship game. Angsman sprinted to two 70-yard touchdowns. Trippi added a 44-yard scoring run and 75-yard punt return for a touchdown.

Angsman finished with 159 rushing yards.

Meanwhile, the defense made three interceptions and held future Hall of Fame running back Steve Van Buren to 1.4 yards per carry. Van Buren had led the NFL in rushing that season, averaging 4.6 yards per carry. And when Cardinals defensive back Marshall Goldberg intercepted a pass from Eagles quarterback Tommy Thompson in the fourth quarter, a 28–21 victory and the title were assured.

"It was a close, hard-fought, rock 'em, sock 'em struggle, with a fair share of thrills," the *New York Times* reported.

The Cardinals gave their fans more than their fair share of thrills in 1948. They won the Western Division title and compiled an 11–1 regular-season

OLLIE'S STORY

The Cardinals certainly struggled in the 1950s. But opponents did have to respect at least one player: running back Ollie Matson.

Matson was selected by the Cardinals in the first round of the 1952 NFL Draft out of the University of San Francisco. The speedy Matson was always the primary target of defenses. But he was unable to turn the Cardinals into winners by himself.

Other NFL teams, however, understood his value. In 1959, the Los Angeles Rams traded a remarkable nine players for him. Matson played for the Cardinals, Rams, Detroit Lions, and Philadelphia Eagles. He finished his career with 12,844 combined rushing, receiving, and return yards, 222 receptions, and 73 touchdowns.

During his 14-year career, he was named to six Pro Bowls. He was inducted into the Pro Football Hall of Fame in 1972.

ARIZONA CARDINALS

record. But the Eagles gained revenge in an NFL Championship Game rematch by shutting them out 7–0.

Conzelman retired that year, and the Cardinals embarked on another long losing spell. They managed just one winning season throughout the 1950s and had a 33–84–3 record during that time.

By that point, owner Violet Bidwill had had enough. She was tired of the losing. She was tired of the Cardinals playing second fiddle in Chicago to the far more popular Bears. And the NFL wanted a team in St. Louis, Missouri, which appeared to be a promising market. The NFL did not want to be beaten to that Midwestern city by the young American Football League. So it gave Bidwill permission to move her team to St. Louis.

A new era in Cardinals football was about to begin.

SLIP-SLIDING AWAY

The Cardinals' last season in Chicago, in 1959, was not a memorable one. They finished the season 2–10 and lost their final six games. They even played two of their home games in Minneapolis, Minnesota. It is no wonder the team moved to St. Louis. In the 15 years after World War II, the Cardinals averaged about 25,000 fans per game in Chicago. They hit rock bottom in 1951, averaging just 17,500 fans per game at home. It was not until the mid-1960s that attendance in St. Louis showed a considerable improvement.

RUNNING BACK OLLIE MATSON WAS A STAR FOR THE CHICAGO CARDINALS IN THE 1950s EVEN THOUGH THE TEAM STRUGGLED.

CHAPTER 4

NEVER QUITE GOOD ENOUGH

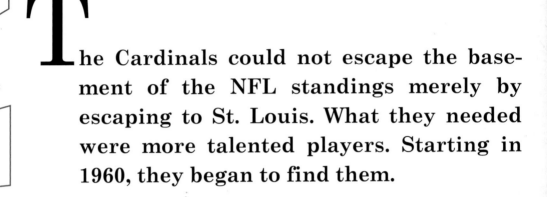

T

he Cardinals could not escape the basement of the NFL standings merely by escaping to St. Louis. What they needed were more talented players. Starting in 1960, they began to find them.

It was in that year that running back John David Crow blossomed into a star. He broke the team single-season record by rushing for 1,071 yards. The Cardinals also drafted running back Larry Wilson, whom they converted into a safety. Wilson quickly developed into one of the finest players in the NFL. And that same year, wide receiver Sonny Randle caught 62 passes, including a league-best 15 for touchdowns.

WONDERFUL WILSON

Who is the best defensive player in Cardinals history? It could very well be safety Larry Wilson. Wilson recorded 52 interceptions for the Cardinals from 1960 to 1972 and led the NFL with 10 in 1966. He earned eight Pro Bowl selections from 1962 to 1970.

OFFENSIVE LINEMAN DAN DIERDORF WAS A STANDOUT FOR THE CARDINALS IN THE 1970s. THE TEAM HAD MOVED TO ST. LOUIS BY THEN, BUT IT CONTINUED TO MOSTLY STRUGGLE.

The Cardinals were no champions. But they proved far better than the teams that were near or at the bottom of the standings in Chicago. It seemed all they needed was a consistent and talented quarterback. And in 1963, they discovered that they had one. His name was Charley Johnson.

Johnson became the full-time starter in 1963 and led the Cardinals to a 9–5 record, their best since 1948. He set four team records that season, including most passing yards (3,280) and

touchdowns (28). Randle and fellow young receiver Bobby Joe Conrad combined for 124 catches, 1,981 yards, and 22 touchdowns. Tight end Jackie Smith, linebacker Larry Stallings, and cornerback Pat Fischer also provided fresh talent.

The Cardinals were soon offered a chance to move to Atlanta. But they remained in St. Louis with the promise of building a new home field. Busch Memorial Stadium opened in 1966 with a capacity of more than 51,000. But the team's play became inconsistent. After Johnson and Fischer, who had 10 interceptions, led the Cardinals to a 9–3–2 record in 1964, they could not sustain a positive trend.

Each winning season in 1964, 1966, 1968, and 1970 was followed by a losing season. When the defense was strong,

WHAT A STEAL!

In 1962, the Cardinals obtained place-kicker Jim Bakken. He had been drafted in the seventh round that same year by the Los Angeles Rams. Little did anyone know that Bakken would blossom into the one of premier kickers in the NFL. He booted the ball for the Cardinals for 17 seasons and led the NFL in field goals made in 1964 and 1967. By the time he hung up his cleats, he had kicked 282 field goals and scored 1,380 points.

WIDE RECEIVER SONNY RANDLE HELPED THE ST. LOUIS CARDINALS
ACHIEVE WINNING RECORDS IN 1960, 1963, 1964, AND 1966.

the offense was not. And when the offense excelled, the defense struggled. But in 1974, the Cardinals put it all together. They won their first seven games and clinched their first playoff berth since 1948. Second-year coach Don Coryell drove the players to have a winning attitude.

"We take nothing for granted now," Smith said after the team

won its first four games. "My first few years here, we'd look at a couple of games as easy, so that we would have a tendency to ease up and slack off. Now it's just impossible to approach a game that way. That's what gives me the best feeling about our potential. That complacent attitude will never be part of this team. Along with that . . . we can get a lot more out of ourselves because we're getting pride and confidence."

Leading the way in 1974 was a new generation of Cardinals. It included quarterback Jim Hart, wide receiver Mel Gray, running backs Terry Metcalf and Jim Otis, defensive back Roger Wehrli, and

CARDINALS TIGHT END JACKIE SMITH MAKES A CATCH IN 1967 AGAINST THE REDSKINS. SMITH, A MEMBER OF THE PRO FOOTBALL HALL OF FAME, PLAYED FOR ST. LOUIS FROM 1963 TO 1977.

DON CORYELL

Until Ken Whisenhunt transformed the Cardinals into NFC champions, the most successful coach in team history was Don Coryell. Coryell was among the NFL's greatest innovators.

Coryell joined the Cardinals after coaching college football at San Diego State. He brought an exciting offensive style to the team with an emphasis on passing.

But it was not until he began coaching the San Diego Chargers in 1978 that he began an era of explosive aerial attacks in the NFL. Among Coryell's strategies was to use the tight end heavily in the passing offense.

The Chargers quickly became one of the most feared offensive teams in the NFL. But his defense was never strong enough to lead to a championship. The defense became so bad that the Chargers began to lose. Coryell quit in 1986.

Pro Bowl offensive linemen Dan Dierdorf and Conrad Dobler.

The Cardinals stumbled badly in the first round of the 1974 playoffs against the Minnesota Vikings. They maintained their momentum by winning 11 of 14 games the next year. But they were dominated again in the playoffs in a 35–23 loss to the Los Angeles Rams.

Coryell left to coach the San Diego Chargers. The Cardinals never recovered in St. Louis. For the third time in their history, they suffered through a long losing stretch. They managed just three winning seasons from 1977 to 1987 and never got close to the playoffs.

The Cardinals did manage a couple good years in the 1980s. In fact, they crept over .500 every season from 1982 to 1984 with one of the best offenses in the NFL. Leading the way were running back Ottis Anderson, quarterback Neil Lomax, and wide receiver Roy Green.

Soon, though, the Cardinals were moving to the desert.

FAILED EXPERIMENT

In 1978, the Cardinals created a buzz by hiring Bud Wilkinson as their coach. Wilkinson had never coached in the NFL. But he had been a highly successful coach at the University of Oklahoma. Wilkinson led an interesting life. After leaving Oklahoma, he dabbled in politics before becoming a college football broadcaster. His two seasons in St. Louis, however, were regrettable. He coached the team to a 9–20 record before stepping down.

OTTIS ANDERSON, SHOWN IN HIS ROOKIE YEAR OF 1979, RUSHED FOR 1,000 YARDS IN FIVE OF HIS FIRST SIX SEASONS FOR THE CARDINALS.

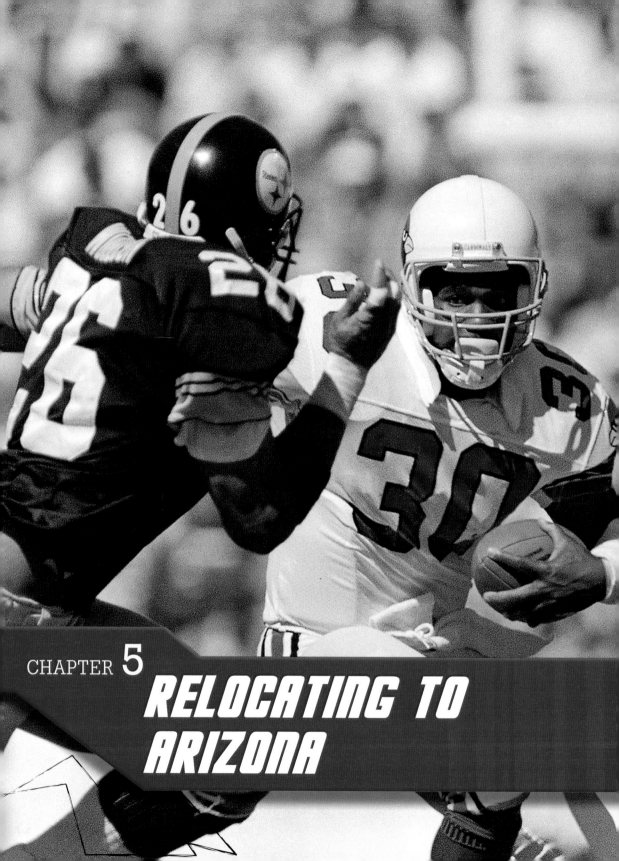

CHAPTER 5

RELOCATING TO ARIZONA

By the late 1980s, Cardinals owner Bill Bidwill, son of Charles and Violet, had become disappointed. Attendance at home games was low. It fell to a meager average of about 28,000 per game in 1987.

Bidwill had been pushing to have a new stadium. He believed it would attract more fans. But he was unable to convince local officials to take the proper steps to have one built. So he moved the team to Arizona. There the team would be known as the Phoenix Cardinals and play at spacious Sun Devil Stadium on the campus of Arizona State University.

St. Louis fans did not show the same outrage that those in other cities, such as Baltimore and later Cleveland, expressed when their NFL teams were taken away. When the *St. Louis Dispatch* newspaper polled fans as to whether they were angrier about the Cardinals leaving or about the departure of Jack Clark from the St. Louis baseball team, the results ended up in a virtual tie.

THE CARDINALS' STUMP MITCHELL RUNS AGAINST THE STEELERS' ROD WOODSON. AFTER MOVING TO PHOENIX IN 1988, THE CARDINALS OFTEN WORE WHITE JERSEYS AT HOME GAMES TO BEAT THE HEAT.

NFL COMMISSIONER PETE ROZELLE, *RIGHT*, AND CARDINALS OWNER BILL BIDWILL ANNOUNCE IN 1988 THAT THE TEAM IS MOVING TO PHOENIX.

The Cardinals did not fare much better in Arizona—at least

SOUTH OF THE BORDER

The Cardinals and San Francisco 49ers made history in 2005 as the first teams to play an NFL regular-season game outside the United States. The contest was held in Mexico City's Estadio Azteca on October 2 before 103,467 fans. It was the largest crowd to witness an NFL regular-season game. And to make matters sweeter for the Cardinals, they won 31–14.

for quite a while. The weather was hot. But the team was not. The Cardinals continued to lose. Their defense remained one of the worst in the NFL for several years. And when the defense showed signs of improvement, the offense collapsed. The team officially changed its name from "Phoenix" Cardinals to "Arizona" Cardinals before the 1994 season. The idea was to show an appreciation for fans from other areas of the state.

Those fans were briefly excited when the team won four of its final five games in 1993 and then hired colorful Buddy Ryan as coach. Attendance jumped significantly in 1994 as the Cardinals won half their games. But they went 4–12 a year later and Ryan lost his job.

Replacement Vince Tobin finally guided the Cardinals to their first winning season in Arizona and a playoff spot in 1998 despite a poor defense. Young quarterback Jake Plummer passed for 3,737 yards, mostly to Frank Sanders and Rob Moore. Those two combined for 2,127 receiving yards. All-Pro cornerback Aeneas Williams shut down the opponent's best receivers.

NEW HOME

In 2000, voters in Maricopa County approved an initiative that would help fund the construction of a new stadium for the Cardinals. The team began play at University of Phoenix Stadium in Glendale, a suburb of Phoenix, in 2006. Through 2009, every game at the stadium was a sellout, with crowds averaging about 64,000. The stadium also hosted the Super Bowl after the 2007 season, won by the New York Giants over the previously unbeaten New England Patriots, 17–14.

The Cardinals were given little chance to win their first-round showdown at Dallas. After all, the Cowboys had beaten them twice in the regular season, including one 38–10 thrashing. But needing a victory to advance, the Cardinals won 20–7. The key to the win was Williams, who shut down star Dallas receiver Michael Irvin.

The Cardinals lost 41–21 to the Minnesota Vikings in the second round of the playoffs. Those who believed the success of 1998 was a sign of things to come were quickly disappointed. The Cardinals slid back into the doldrums, going 41–87 without a winning season from 1999 to 2006.

By 2005, however, the combination of quarterback Kurt Warner and wide receivers Larry Fitzgerald and Anquan Boldin had begun giving NFL pass defenses fits.

The Cardinals went 5-11 in both 2005 and 2006. But they improved to 8–8 in 2007. Warner threw for 27 touchdowns that season. Fitzgerald had 100 catches for 1,409 yards and 10 touchdowns. Boldin added 71 receptions for 853 yards and nine touchdowns.

Then came the thrill of the 2008 season. Arizona's passing attack became even stronger. Warner threw for 4,583 yards and 30 touchdowns. Wide receivers Fitzgerald, Boldin, and Steve Breaston each had 1,000 receiving yards. The Cardinals' defense struggled in the regular season. But the unit played well enough in the playoffs to help the team make the surprise run to the Super Bowl. The Cardinals lost 27–23 to the Pittsburgh Steelers in Super Bowl XLIII. But Arizona was understandably excited about its prospects for 2009.

CARDINALS SAFETY PAT TILLMAN TAKES A BREAK IN 2001. TILLMAN ENLISTED IN THE U.S. ARMY IN 2002 AND DIED IN 2004 SERVING IN AFGHANISTAN.

DONE? NO WAY

Some believed Cardinals quarterback Kurt Warner was through as a starting quarterback heading into 2007. He proved his skeptics wrong.

Warner was one of the finest quarterbacks in the NFL from 1999 to 2001. He led the St. Louis Rams to a Super Bowl title in the first of those three seasons. But he had been hampered by injuries and poor performances since 2002.

He performed well in 2007, however, and then brilliantly in 2008 and 2009. Warner led the Cardinals to the NFC championship and earned a Pro Bowl spot in 2008. He then threw for 3,753 yards and 26 touchdowns in 2009 before announcing his retirement in January 2010.

Warner finished his career with 32,344 passing yards and 208 touchdowns. Upon his retirement, he was considered a strong candidate for the Pro Football Hall of Fame.

The Cardinals continued to feature an exciting passing attack led by Warner, Fitzgerald, and Boldin that season. Arizona went 10–6 and won its second straight NFC West title.

The Cardinals played host to the Green Bay Packers in a playoff wild-card game. Arizona pulled out a 51–45 victory in overtime in the highest-scoring game in NFL playoff history. Warner was nearly flawless, outdueling Packers quarterback Aaron Rodgers. Warner completed 29 of 33 pass attempts for 379 yards and five touchdowns. The Cardinals won when linebacker Karlos Dansby returned a fumble by Rodgers 17 yards for a

KURT WARNER THROWS A PASS IN NOVEMBER 2008. WARNER PLAYED HIS FINAL FIVE SEASONS WITH ARIZONA AND LED THE TEAM TO A SUPER BOWL BEFORE HE RETIRED IN JANUARY 2010.

touchdown. "Whew," Warner said at a news conference after the game. "Anybody else tired?"

The Cardinals were overwhelmed the next week in a 45–14 road loss to the New Orleans Saints. The Saints would go on to win the Super Bowl.

Warner announced his retirement from the NFL on January 29, 2010, at the age of 38. He had played 12 seasons in the league. Warner was not drafted by any NFL team after he had completed his college career at the University of Northern Iowa. He held a job stocking the shelves at a grocery store in Iowa before the St. Louis Rams gave him a shot in the late 1990s. His career then took off.

"It's been an amazing ride," Warner said at the news conference in which he announced his retirement. "I don't think I could have dreamt it would have played out like it has, but I've been humbled every day."

Warner's departure created uncertainty about whether Arizona would continue to succeed. But he had shown that the long-suffering Cardinals were capable of soaring to great heights.

THAT'S A LOT OF YARDS!

From the 2005 season through 2009, Cardinals players exceeded 1,000 receiving yards nine times. Larry Fitzgerald and Anquan Boldin both enjoyed four 1,000-yard seasons during that period. Steve Breaston added another in 2008.

KARLOS DANSBY CELEBRATES HIS FUMBLE-RETURN TOUCHDOWN THAT GAVE ARIZONA A 51–45 PLAYOFF WIN OVER GREEN BAY IN JANUARY 2010.

TIMELINE

1898	A football team later known as the Cardinals is formed and plays in Chicago.
1901	The team is purchased by painting and decorating contractor Chris O'Brien and adopts its current nickname.
1917	The Cardinals win the Chicago Football League title.
1920	The franchise joins the American Professional Football League, which becomes the National Football League (NFL) in 1922.
1925	The Cardinals clinch the NFL title on December 12 by virtue of their 11–2–1 record.
1932	The team is bought by Charles W. Bidwill. The move marks the beginning of family ownership that still stood as of 2010.
1947	The Cardinals earn their only win in an NFL Championship Game with a 28–21 victory over the Philadelphia Eagles in Chicago on December 28.
1948	The team plays in its second consecutive league title game but falls to the Eagles in Philadelphia, 7–0 on December 19.
1956	The Cardinals finish 7–5 for their only winning season in the 1950s. The team will go 33–84–3 during the decade.

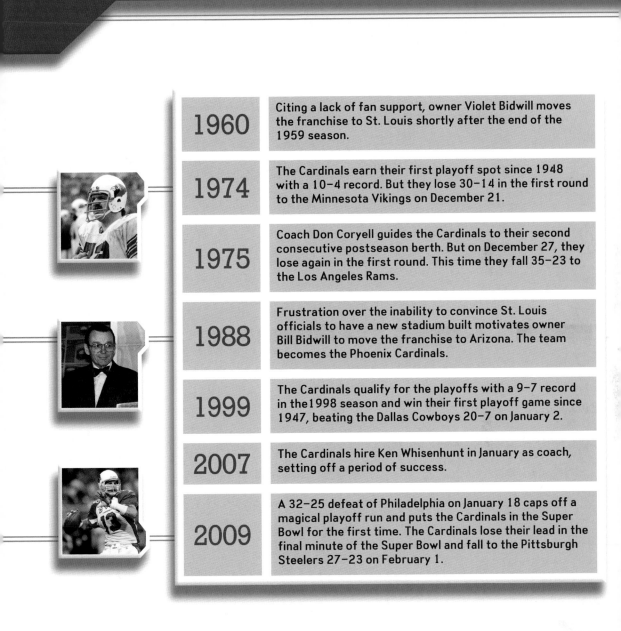

1960	Citing a lack of fan support, owner Violet Bidwill moves the franchise to St. Louis shortly after the end of the 1959 season.
1974	The Cardinals earn their first playoff spot since 1948 with a 10–4 record. But they lose 30–14 in the first round to the Minnesota Vikings on December 21.
1975	Coach Don Coryell guides the Cardinals to their second consecutive postseason berth. But on December 27, they lose again in the first round. This time they fall 35–23 to the Los Angeles Rams.
1988	Frustration over the inability to convince St. Louis officials to have a new stadium built motivates owner Bill Bidwill to move the franchise to Arizona. The team becomes the Phoenix Cardinals.
1999	The Cardinals qualify for the playoffs with a 9–7 record in the 1998 season and win their first playoff game since 1947, beating the Dallas Cowboys 20–7 on January 2.
2007	The Cardinals hire Ken Whisenhunt in January as coach, setting off a period of success.
2009	A 32–25 defeat of Philadelphia on January 18 caps off a magical playoff run and puts the Cardinals in the Super Bowl for the first time. The Cardinals lose their lead in the final minute of the Super Bowl and fall to the Pittsburgh Steelers 27–23 on February 1.

QUICK STATS

FRANCHISE HISTORY
Racine Cardinals (1920–21)
Chicago Cardinals (1922–59)
St. Louis Cardinals (1960–87)
Phoenix Cardinals (1988–93)
Arizona Cardinals (1994–)

SUPER BOWLS
2008 (XLIII)

NFL CHAMPIONSHIP GAMES
(1933–69; wins in bold)
1947, 1948

NFC CHAMPIONSHIP GAMES
(since 1970 AFL-NFL merger)
2008

DIVISION CHAMPIONSHIPS
(since 1970 AFL-NFL merger)
1974, 1975, 2008, 2009

KEY PLAYERS
(position, seasons with team)
Ottis Anderson (RB, 1979–86)
Dan Dierdorf (OT, 1971–83)
Larry Fitzgerald (WR, 2004–)
Jim Hart (QB, 1966–83)
Dick "Night Train" Lane
    (CB, 1954–59)
Ollie Matson (RB, 1952, 1954–58)
Ernie Nevers (FB, 1929–31)
Jackie Smith (TE, 1963–77)
Charley Trippi (RB-QB, 1947–55)
Kurt Warner (QB, 2005–09)
Aeneas Williams (CB, 1991–2000)
Larry Wilson (S, 1960–72)

KEY COACHES
Jimmy Conzelman (1940–42;
    1946–48): 34–31–3; 1–1 (playoffs)
Ken Whisenhunt (2007–):
    27–21–0; 4–2 (playoffs)

HOME FIELDS
University of Phoenix Stadium
    (2006–)
Sun Devil Stadium (1988–2005)
Busch Stadium (1966–87)
Sportsman's Park (1960–65)
Soldier Field (1959)
Comiskey Park (1922–25, 1929–58)
Normal Field (1920–21, 1926–28)

* All statistics through 2009 season

QUOTES AND ANECDOTES

The Chicago Cardinals lost so many players to military service during World War II that they were forced to merge with the Pittsburgh Steelers to form one club in 1944. Despite the fact that they combined two teams, the Cardinals continued to struggle. They still lost all 10 games that season.

For a short time in the early- and mid-1960s, the NFL paired up the two teams that finished second in their respective divisions for a game titled the "Playoff Bowl." The Cardinals placed second in their division in 1964 and defeated the Green Bay Packers 24–17 in the Playoff Bowl on January 3, 1965.

Dan Dierdorf, an NFL Hall of Famer who was perhaps the greatest offensive lineman in Cardinals history, went on to a sterling career as a color commentator on NFL television broadcasts. He served for many years on the *Monday Night Football* crew in the 1980s and 1990s.

The Cardinals enjoyed one of their finest seasons in St. Louis in 1976. But one game that season proved quite embarrassing. They set an NFL record by losing eight fumbles in a game at Washington. It comes as no surprise that they lost 20–10.

Most running backs run the ball far more often than they catch it. Such was not the case with Cardinals back Larry Centers, who was a pass-catching specialist. Centers racked up an amazing 101 receptions for 962 yards in 1995. In the process, he became the first NFL running back to catch more than 100 passes in a season.

GLOSSARY

archrival

An opponent that brings out great emotion in a team and its players.

disband

To break up, as in a sports franchise.

elite

A player or team that is among the best.

franchise

An entire sports organization, including the players, coaches, and staff.

hall of fame

A place built to honor noteworthy achievements by athletes in their respective sports.

innovative

Being creative in doing things a new way, generally with positive results.

laughingstock

That which is greatly disrespected to the point of being a joke.

market

The city in which a team plays.

overshadow

To outshine or surpass.

Pro Bowl

A game after the regular season in which the top players from the AFC play against the top players from the NFC.

respectable

Highly regarded or well thought of.

retire

To officially end one's career.

rookie

A first-year professional athlete.

showdown

An important game.

FOR MORE INFORMATION

Further Reading

Sports Illustrated. *The Football Book Expanded Edition*. New York: Sports Illustrated Books, 2009.

Triumph Books. *Desert Storm: Kurt Warner and the Arizona Cardinals' Unforgettable Run to the Super Bowl*. Chicago: Triumph Books, 2009.

Ziemba, Joe. *When Football Was Football: The Chicago Cardinals and the Birth of the NFL*. Chicago: Triumph Books, 1999.

Web Links

To learn more about the Arizona Cardinals, visit ABDO Publishing Company online at **www.abdopublishing.com**. Web sites about the Cardinals are featured on our Book Links page. These links are routinely monitored and updated to provide the most current information available.

Places to Visit

Arizona Cardinals Training Camp
Pine Ridge Village
Northern Arizona University
Flagstaff, AZ 86011
928-523-1818
Cardinals practices are free and open to the public. Parking is also free.

Pro Football Hall of Fame
2121 George Halas Drive Northwest
Canton, OH 44708
330-456-8207
www.profootballhof.com
This hall of fame and museum highlights the greatest players and moments in the history of the National Football League. As of 2010, 17 people affiliated with the Cardinals were enshrined. They included Dan Dierdorf, Ollie Matson, Ernie Nevers, and Larry Wilson.

University of Phoenix Stadium
One Cardinals Drive
Glendale, AZ 85305
602-379-0101
www.azcardinals.com/stadium/index.html
This is where the Cardinals play all their home games.

INDEX

About the Author

Marty Gitlin is a freelance writer based in Cleveland, Ohio. He has written more than 25 educational books. He lives with his wife and three children.